MW00326169

40 DAYS

of Praise from Prison

NATHAN STORM

ISBN 978-1-63903-491-8 (paperback)
ISBN 978-1-63903-492-5 (digital)

Copyright © 2022 by Nathan Storm

All rights reserved. No part of this publication may be reproduced, distributed, or transmitted in any form or by any means, including photocopying, recording, or other electronic or mechanical methods without the prior written permission of the publisher. For permission requests, solicit the publisher via the address below.

Christian Faith Publishing
832 Park Avenue
Meadville, PA 16335
www.christianfaithpublishing.com

Printed in the United States of America

Intro to *40 Days of Praise in Prison*

First of all, I want to thank God for all he does for me. This has been a very trying year with COVID-19, social injustice, and political scandals. It has been especially tough for those who are in prison. We have been on lockdown almost an entire year. I don't wish this situation on anyone, but it is real, and it has been a test of my faith. I don't know how others have maintained their sanity, but I have leaned on our Lord and Savior Jesus Christ. My relationship has grown stronger throughout the year, and every day I pray, read the Bible, and just hope that he will make a way for all the men and their families who are also suffering with us. This book was written just to show thanks for all God does in my life and that we owe all the glory to him. I hope that if you are reading this, you can take some inspiration and hope that God has a plan for us all. If you put a place for Jesus in your heart, God will put a place for you in his eternal kingdom.

Opening Prayer for My Brother Will, Thank You for All You Do

God,

I need you to hear this prayer to you today. We need you more than ever, Lord, right now.

Please help the sick and weak, those unable to care for themselves. They are children of God, and they need your help. I ask in the name of Jesus that whoever calls on your name this day, you answer their prayers if they align with your great plan. Thank you for reminding me where my foundation is. The blood of Jesus is the salvation for the world. Let us not forget that. Use me today to bring someone or someones to the light so they can rejoice and glorify your name. Please look on Will today with favor if he calls for help in your name. I humbly ask for you to use me and my temple to spread your message and make me a light to shine for others to follow. I love you and give you all the honor, glory, and power in Jesus's name. Amen.

BEGINNING OF 40 DAYS

First Day

John 12:44–49

Dear Lord,

Thank you for all you do, especially for your Son, Jesus Christ, who came to save the world and allows me and the rest of us to speak to you through him. We need you right now more than ever as this world is suffering through sickness, sin, and injustices that seem to grow daily. Only you are the answer to the problems of this world you created, and only you have the solution. Help me and the rest of the world listen to the message of your Son, Jesus, so that we can walk in peace and love. I pray for the world, for my family, and most of all for you. Thank you, Father, for I ask all this in Jesus Christ's name.

Amen.

Second Day

John 3:16–18

Dear Lord,

Thank you for sending your Son, Jesus, to save the world. Forgive us for not taking your gift of salvation but destroying it. Please come into our hearts today and let us be led by the fruits of the spirit so that we may follow your Son's example. Please put a hedge of protection on those who are sick, in danger, and seeking salvation. Let them follow your Son, Jesus, so that he may be glorified and you will be honored as it should be. I ask this in Christ's name.
Amen.

Third Day

Psalm 71

Lord, help me from my enemies. May their plans and conspiring be thwarted by your mercy and godliness. Pray for those who are broken and contrite of heart and spirit. Remember all those who are lost on this Memorial Day and pray for their families to find comfort in you, Lord. I cannot express my fears or doubts in people and their actions, but in you I will trust. Deliver me from my enemies and fill their hearts with love instead of hate. I ask all this in Jesus Christ's name.

Amen.

Fourth Day

John 12

Dear Lord,

Today I want to die, not in the literal sense, but the spiritual. Wash away my old sinful nature and let me blossom into a child of you, the Most High God. The old may be replaced with the fruits of the spirit working for your glory and to bring others to know you through your precious Son, Jesus Christ. Thank you so much for all you do in my life.

Amen.

Fifth Day

Jeremiah 31:3
Luke 11

Dear Eloi,

I thank you for speaking to my heart this morning. May my supplications be heard, and may I fulfill the promises I made to you. I know that I'm forgiven for my sins and have been redeemed by the blood of Jesus Christ, your Son. I offer myself as a living sacrifice to testify about your Son, Jesus; and if I may be so bold, I place myself in your service. This comes from my heart and not for selfish reasons. You know that just as you know the number of hairs on my head and the number of stars in the sky, and you know my heart. Test me, Lord, for I am ready to be your humble servant. I ask in Jesus's name. Amen.

Sixth Day

Eloi,

Today, I ask for strength, strength to do your will for my life and for others. When I struggle with dark forces, it is you who give me courage. Sometimes I feel your presence more than other times. The spirit in me feels weak. Have I done something to anger you? Please use the spirit today in others so they can feel your power and your love. Let them who are of contrite spirit be helped, and let there be peace for them. Thank you, Jesus, today.

Amen.

Seventh Day

Heavenly Father,

Thank you for allowing me to come to you today and worship you. Thank you for your Son, Jesus Christ, whom you sent down as a living sacrifice for us. Without him my supplications to you would not be possible. Let me learn to produce fruits that are pleasing to you and an example of Christ our Lord. Thank you for your protection and for your love. In Jesus Christ's name, I give you the glory and my love. Thank you, Eloi.
Selah.

Eighth Day

Ephesians 4:17–32

Dear Lord,

Please forgive me for the doubts. I realize that is fear that causes me not to believe. Satan tries to destroy my relationship with you because he knows that he can; but there is your Son, Jesus Christ, whom you sent to me as an example that we can, as believers in him, overcome dark forces and spiritual wickedness. I humbly ask you to come into my heart today and give me the peace and love that can come only from believing in your Word and your Son, Jesus Christ. Let the old man be put off and the renewed spirit of God dwell inside me. All this I receive in the name of Jesus. Thank you, Father God, for all you do. Please look after all those who are dealing with the floods and fires that are taking place right now. In Jesus's name, I pray.
Amen.

Ninth Day

Proverbs 18:10

God is
- the Shepherd who guides (Jehovah-raah),
- the Lord who provides (Jehovah-jireh),
- the Voice who brings peace in the storm (Jehovah-shalom),
- the Physician who heals the sick (Jehovah-rophe), and
- the Banner that guides the soldier (Jehovah-nissi).

God, you have so many names and are so glorious and merciful. Thank you for all that you do and all that you are. Please fill our hearts today with love and patience we need as we wait on Jesus Christ, our Lord, who is love.

Amen.

Tenth Day

Philippians 1

Dear Lord,

Thanks be to you for your mercy and for the work you are doing in my life. Let me glorify your name with praise and love. Allow me to share the message of Jesus Christ to others. Let me tell the truth about the coming of our Lord and Savior, Jesus. Please send your words to me today through the Comforter, and I will boldly and proudly give his message to others, if that is your will. Thank you for being my refuge in these trying times. I love you and just want to honor you in however you see fit for the plans in my life.
Amen.

Eleventh Day

Matthew 7:1–6

Heavenly Father,

Thank you for your words, guidance, and love. Thank you for your Son, Jesus Christ, who teaches us about judging others. Please help me today and all the rest of my days to be helpful and not hurtful to others. Let me be first to speak with love, not hate or criticism. I pray for all those who pass judgment without realizing it is God who does that, not us. Let them be filled with the grace of God. Jesus, open my eyes to your words and let me speak truth and love with my mouth and let my ears hear what is good and shut out what is evil. I ask this in the name of Jesus.
Amen.

Twelfth Day

2 Thessalonians 3:1–5

Jehovah,

Direct our hearts to the patient waiting of our Lord, Jesus Christ. Let not the believers be led to the wicked men with their schemes and deception. I call on you to put love into their hearts and let them be filled with peace. Thank you for your instructions and your messages from the Holy Spirit who leads me into the path of righteousness. Let me do your will and give hope to those who are hopeless. Give me power to overcome those who persecute your name, and lead me today in the ways to glorify your name. I pray for all the men of this place and their families and for all the world to return to your Son, Jesus.
Amen.

Thirteenth Day

1 Peter 5:8–9

Dear Lord,

Please help us today walk in the path that Christ wants for us. May we be covered by the blood of the Lamb who is our Protector and Deliverer. I ask that you protect me from my enemies and protect my enemies and their families from harm and sickness. Let this day be a day of healing and restoration, not anger and destruction. May I help just one person come to you today, dear Lord, so they may be filled with the spirit. In Jesus's name, I ask.

Amen.

Fourteenth Day

Matthew 15

Dear Lord,

Thank you for all that you do. May my heart be filled with the Holy Spirit and be an example of your love and grace. I ask for your help and protection for all those who seek you and call on your name, the Lord Jesus Christ.
Amen.

Fifteenth Day

Hebrews 13

Dear Lord,

Thank you for this day and the chance to fellowship with you through the Holy Spirit with prayer and from reading your words. May I do your will and not mine. Let my words and actions be to glorify you, dear Lord. Forgive me of my trespasses and let me forgive others and make my heart pure so that I may be an example for the way your Son, Jesus Christ, intended us to be. All my love and strength comes from you, so I thank you. Thank you for all the people you have put in my life who have led me down the path to you.
Amen.

Sixteenth Day

Psalm 92

Thank you, God. I know that you are working in my life for the greater good to glorify you. Thank you for opening my eyes to the things that matter in this world. I humbly ask to be filled with the Holy Spirit to help me and do your will. Thank you for all the officials, wards, and prisoners here at this facility. May their hearts be filled with your grace and mercy. Let them feel your love, God, and protect them from evil and their families as well. Thank you for giving me hope and peace. Most of all, thank you for your Son, Jesus Christ.

Amen.

Seventeenth Day

Dear Lord,

Thanks and praise to you on this day. Help me follow the instructions you have set for us through your Word and through the life of your Son, Jesus. Thank you, Jesus, for your love and your help today as we struggle with sin and health issues. Let me glorify you in all that I do.

Amen.

Eighteenth Day

Eloi,

Today I want to follow your commandments, especially the commandment to love. Let your spirit work through me today to show care and compassion to those who are in need. Let me do your will for your glory and not for selfish reasons. I ask that you put love in the hearts of all today. Let them know how it feels to be loved by you. Thank you for all you do for me.

Amen.

Nineteenth Day

Revelation 3:20

Dear I Am,

Thank you for all you do when we don't deserve. Thank you for your love when we are filled with hate. Thank you for your mercy when we do not forgive. May the teachings and the way of your Son, Jesus Christ, be an example of what you want for us and for our way to live. May the Holy Spirit fill us with love, peace, and kindness today to glorify your name.
Amen.

Twentieth Day

Bencao Pai,

Today as we go on, please bless us and let us know your presence. Thank you for all the gifts you give us. Thank you for your Son, Jesus Christ. Thank you for the Holy Spirit who fills us. That is, you are the I Am in everything. How wonderful it is to feel your love in all creation. I ask that I can be that love you give to others. Protect us from sin and keep us in health. Cover us in love.

Amen.

Twenty-First Day

Romans 12

Heavenly Father,

I ask you today to put us in unity according to your Word. May we agree in fellowship and love for the one true sovereign, Jesus Christ. Open our eyes and our hearts as we go through this day. Amen.

Twenty-Second Day

1 John 4

Dear Lord,

Thank you for your undying love. Thank you for showing me your wonderful power. Thank you for the Holy Spirit who is in me and who is you. Every day my eyes are opened up to the mysteries of the gospel, and everyday I'm left in wonderful amazement. You have given me so much. Thank you for your mercy and grace. Lift my head up in times of trouble and give me strength from the spirit. Let me love my brother as you love me.
Amen.

Twenty-Third Day

Romans 13

Dear Lord,

Help us be obedient to the power of goodness and help us shun evil. Let the authorities in control be working for the greater good, which is faith in the coming of Jesus Christ. Let us not be dismayed or falter to the evil forces that wait to trip us up. Let us be faithful to Christ as he has been faithful to us. Thank you for this day.
Amen.

Twenty-Fourth Day

Matthew 14

Dear Jesus,

Thank you for being there for us when we falter or fail. When our faith is diminished and we are weak, you are there to help us. Your gift of salvation is all we need even when we don't realize. It's not by our works but by yours that we are saved. Help us today remember your sacrifice and your message to love one another and to be kind to our brothers and sisters. Let me do what I can for whom I can when I can.

Amen.

Twenty-Fifth Day

Dear Lord,

Give me strength and patience that is for the greater good for your glory and for my brothers. Let me not be persuaded or falter to evil and let me be strong with courage and righteousness. Bless me with the spirit to do your will and let me lift up others around me for good and not evil. Thank you for all you do for me, and I pray for everyone here at this facility and their families. Keep them safe, and I look toward you and your glory.

Amen.

Twenty-Sixth Day

John 15

Dear Heavenly Father,

I need you for everything in my life. Help me today to live for your glory and not mine. Forgive me for my trespasses against others as they forgive me. Let us walk in love and the fruits of the spirit today. I want to ask you to help those in need, those who are sick, and those who are lost. Let them begin to know salvation through your Son, Jesus Christ. Make me a light in the darkness and let me help you help me bring the good news to this world.
Amen.

Twenty-Seventh Day

1 John 4

Dear Heavenly Father,

Thank you for your undying love. Help us today as we face another challenge. Give me strength to do your will. In the Bible it says when we walk in the love of God, it is without fear and it is not burdensome. Let me feel at peace as I do your will to glorify your name. Let me honor you by spreading the Word to others who may be broken and hurt. There is a time coming when you will call on me to do your will. Let me be able to hear and answer that call and to do your calling in the name of Jesus Christ our Lord and Savior.
Amen.

Twenty-Eighth Day

Colossians 1
Psalm 91

Heavenly Father,

I want to pray today for others. Let them be filled with the Holy Spirit. Let them walk in faith and not fear. May they carry the message of Jesus in the midst of suffering and turmoil. Lift their heads up toward you and fill them with your light and remove the darkness and pestilence in their lives. Lord, thank you for all that you do to protect us with your power, your words, and most of all your Son, Jesus. I ask that you put your mighty wings over those who call you today and those who are lost into your loving arms of protection. I ask this in Jesus's name.
Amen.

Twenty-Ninth Day

Psalm 104:31

Elohim,

Thank you for your marvelous gifts and creations. Thank you for letting us take the time to realize your omnipresence and your works. I ask that you enter all the hearts who seek you today and call on your name. May they be filled with the spirit and be thankful to your grace and mercy. I want to ask you today in the name of Jesus to take my life for your good and to do your works. Please hear my prayers as we go through these difficult times in the world and this prison. May the men not be forgotten just because they have been sentenced by earthly judges and not the one true Judge. Thank you for the light you have brought on this day.
Amen.

Thirtieth Day

Elohim,

Thank you for never turning away from me after I have turned away from you. Thank you for opening my eyes and my heart to you, Lord. Let me pray for those who do not believe and forgive those who trespass against me. Please let me lean on your understanding and trust in you and not in my own sinful ways. I ask that you help me with all this in Jesus Christ's name.

Amen.

Thirty-First Day

Adonai,

Today, let the spirit of the Lord come into prison—into the officials, the prison cells, and most of all the hearts of the men who are incarcerated here. Dear Lord, we have been through so much for so long. Please open the hearts and minds of the officials to show mercy and compassion for the injustice that has been done. Only you have the right, God, not the warden, the captain, or the guards who are keeping us captive. Lift up the spirits of the men here and let them know they are not alone. You are with them, dear Lord. I am with them in spirit, body, and love. Thank you for your Son, Jesus, and may he hear my supplications and change the hearts of everyone here at this prison. All I do, I do for you.

Amen.

Thirty-Second Day

Psalm 27

My Lord,

Thank you for being a light of hope. In the midst of all this, you are there. Sometimes it's hard to believe in the plan you have for us, but that is why it is called faith. We believe in you and your love and patiently wait for the coming of Jesus. While we wait, let us do your will and glorify your name. Let us love one another even when it is not easy or pleasant to do so. I ask that you put love in the hearts of those who do not believe, faith in those who do not have patience, and peace in those who are in calamity and chaos. Open their eyes and hearts. I ask this in Jesus's name.

Amen.

Thirty-Third Day

Titus 3:4–6

Dear God,

Today let us worship your grace and mercy by honoring you for the greatest gift we could ever receive, Jesus. Your Son made it possible for us to come to you with our prayers and requests. He is our High Priest for all time, every day, forever. That is something to be grateful for. Today, I ask in Jesus's name that you remove indifference and bond us with unity and love. Let us all walk in light and not darkness. This has gone on too long, here at this prison and in this world. Let the rulers and authorities be given the solutions by listening to the spirit of God and not their own subversive reasons. Please look over all the families and men here during the continuation of these stressful times. I ask in your Son's name.
Amen.

Thirty-Fourth Day

Isaiah 56

Dear Lord,

Today let us remain faithful in your Word. Let the spirit fill our hearts with love and truth. Help us lift up our brothers and give them encouragement and strength. Allow me to be a guide to you, my Lord. Help me help you. I know you don't need help, but I do, and so do others here. I ask for protection for my family today. Let them be filled with joy and peace. Give me strength and courage to do your will. I ask all this in Jesus's name.

Amen.

Thirty-Fifth Day

Ephesians 6
Psalm 23

Lord,

Thank you for this day. Seventy-one years ago, you created my mother. She is the reason I came to you after being lost for so long. She truly was my shepherd. She protected me, fed me, and clothed me. Most of all she loved me, unconditionally. You have taken her to a better place, so I thank you. Let her continue her work for you in heaven. I ask that you keep her and comfort her with blessings and love just as she did for me. Today is a day to celebrate a life that was an example of faith, love, and courage. I only hope to grow into the same-caliber servant for God that she was. I will always love you, Mary Elaine Storm. Until we meet again, I will carry on your love and faith in the Lord.

Amen.

Thirty-Sixth Day

Daniel 9:15–23

God,

You live in all of us through the spirit. Let us not forget that you are working through us to do your will. Thank you for your mercy. Let me not forget your grace is a gift and not something I have earned. Please help me to live in accordance to your will. May I help to bring others to know you and your wonderful Son. May the fruits of the spirit be passed on through me to the others in my life. Your precious gift is to be shared by all. I am asking today in the name of Jesus that you lead me on the path of righteousness and let me be a part of your wonderful kingdom. You are truly the Father of all who see you, and I am proud to call you mine. Thank you for this day, and bless and protect these men and their families.

Amen.

Thirty-Seventh Day

Revelation 19:11–16

Adonai,

Thank you for saving us. Thank you for your sacrifice so that we may have eternal life. Let our faith grow in you as a mustard seed grows into moving mountains (Matthew 17:20). Dear Lord, when you come back to judge the world, I pray that everyone has been saved and follows you. May we be part of your army when you ride on the battlefield of Armageddon in Megiddo. Lord, we need no weapons as long as you are by our side. You will protect us and keep us because of our faith. You are the King of kings and Lord of lords. Thank you for your agape. It is all we need in this world. Help me today to do what I can for your will and your plan. Thank you for all you do.

Amen.

Thirty-Eighth Day

Romans

For all have sinned and come short of the glory of God. But God commandeth his love toward us in that, while we were yet sinners, Christ died for us for the wages of sin is death: but the gift of God is eternal life through Jesus Christ our Lord that if thou shalt confess with thy mouth the Lord Jesus and shalt believe in thine heart that God hath raised him from the dead, thou shalt be saved. For with the heart man believeth unto righteousness; and with the mouth confession is made unto salvation. For whosoever shall call upon the name of the Lord shall be saved.

Dear Lord,

Thank you for your Son, Jesus Christ. May we never forget the sacrifice made for all humanity. Let us rejoice in our Lord and Savior and practice humanity and kindness for the sake of goodness and righteousness. I ask that you enter the hearts of the men at this prison and give them peace and faith that is in our Lord Jesus Christ. Thank you for all you do.
Amen.

Thirty-Ninth Day

Heavenly Father,

I want to thank you for all that you do in my life. Thank you for my health, my family, and most of all, your wonderful Son, Jesus. May we take time each day to appreciate this wonderful world and all the great things in it. Not everything is bad. Not everything is broken. Hope is not lost, as long as we keep our focus on the important things—kindness, family, love, and most of all you, God. I am so thankful to be able to wake up each day and start a new day with you—time to meditate, time to relax, and time to strengthen our relationship. Father God, it's the highlight of my day. Let me not forget what's important to you. Bless this prison and all the inmates and staff and let us all wake up tomorrow and place you first in our lives.

Amen.

Fortieth Day

Dear God,

I just want to pray for all the men at FCI Beaumont. I want to pray for their families. Dear Lord, I want to ask you to heal those who are sick, those who are depressed, and those who are battling addiction. Heavenly Father, you say to stand on your Word and trust that you have a plan. Well, let those who don't feel like they are part of your plan find purpose today that is given from you. We are all struggling. And this is very tough, dear Lord, the way we are forced to live. May the authorities who are in charge be given the fruits of the spirit and follow the attitude of Jesus. We are praying for change, dear Lord, that is going to have to come from you. I ask all this in the name of Jesus.

Amen.

Extra Day One

Psalm 138:7

Lord,

Even when I have trouble all around me, you will keep me alive.

Dear Heavenly Father,

You have ominous power, yet you never abuse it. Help me today to have discipline and control of my life. Instead of my will, help me to make it your will. You could control all our thoughts, yet you give us a choice. Help me to choose wisely and always think of you, Heavenly Father, and my brothers before I think of myself. Please keep us safe on this day as we praise and worship you.
Amen.

Extra Day Two

Mark 7

Dear Lord,

I ask that you give me strength today to be a better Christian. Let my faith not falter or be hypocritical. May I stand on your words of truth, and let them be the example for my life. Father, I want to thank you for your protection, guidance, and love. Without you, my world is lost. Let me find patience and comfort in your words and walk in faith and not by sight. I owe all I am to you, Lord. Thank you for always being there for me. If there is anything I can do, I ask that you direct my path. Thank you for your Son, Jesus Christ. Please be with us during these difficult times.

Amen.

Extra Day Three

Luke 15:10

Dear Lord,

Thank you for this day. Even though it is hard and I'm finding it tough, I am still thankful. Thank you for my wonderful family. May you bless them today and let them feel joy. I ask that you be with me and keep me looking toward you and not my situation. Give us all strength and feed us and shelter us with your Word and with your power. Let us not fall into temptation and put ourselves back on the path. I ask this in Jesus's name.
Amen.

Extra Day Four

2 Corinthians 5

Dear Lord,

Sometimes we feel insignificant and unworthy, but you and Jesus always are there to make us feel needed. I know that I should be more thankful for this love, and sometimes I get into my worldly self and think I need more. We never need anything but Jesus. He is the only comfort that matters. Thank you for helping me realize my sacrifice is nothing compared to his. Let me not forget it was his love for me that has made my salvation possible. Let me walk with pride and joy knowing he is on my side. Please watch over my family and the men here at this facility and their families. All the glory to you, my Lord.
Amen.

Extra Day Five

God,

Help me today to understand your plan. Help me to continue to believe and have faith when all seems hopeless. Let me believe that you are working in my life when I don't seem to understand. Please allow me to be considerate, kind, and patient as I struggle through this place. I ask for strength, in the name of Jesus.

Amen.

For God so loved the world that he gave his only begotten Son and whosoever shall believe on Him shall not perish but have everlasting life. (John 3:16)

"Come, Thou Fount of Every Blessing"

Tune my heart to sing thy grace,
Streams of mercy, never ceasing
Call for songs of loudest praise.
Teach me some melodious songs
Sung by flaming tongues above.
Praise the mount, I'm fixed upon it,
Mount of thy redeeming love.

Sorrowing I shall be in spirit,
Till released from flesh and sin,
Yet what I do inherit here thy praises I'll being
Here I raise my Ebenezer
Hereby great help I've come
And I hope by thy good pleasure,
Safely to arrive at home.

Ebenezer means "stone of help."
Lord, you want me to look for your help every day until I am with you in heaven. Thank you so much for all your help thus far.
Amen.

About the Author

Nathan Storm grew up in West Texas. He played sports and made good grades. He was introduced to alcohol and drugs in his early teens and has battled addiction since. In November of 2018, he was sentenced to 270 months in federal prison for drugs. He is currently serving that sentence in a federal correctional institution in Texas. He is kind, positive, smart, and beloved by his family. Nathan loves the Lord and others. He is currently waiting on a miracle not only for himself but the masses serving unfair prison sentences for drug addiction.